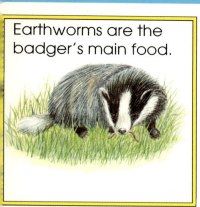
Earthworms are the badger's main food.

Cubs outside their underground ...ett.

Footprints

Badger

Badgers live in family groups in quiet woods. They come out at night. Look for worn tracks leading to their setts.

Hedgehogs eat worms,
beetles and slugs.

Mother with her young,
usually four or five.

Hedgehogs roll up into
a spiny ball if attacked.

Hedgehog

These are night animals. They
sleep through the winter in a
nest of leaves. They are often
seen in gardens.

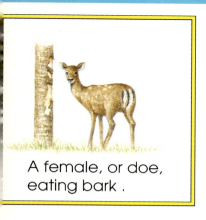

A female, or doe, eating bark .

A baby deer is called a fawn.

Male, or buck

Fallow deer

These deer like to live where there is plenty of grass to eat, and trees and bushes to hide them.

Eating an acorn.

Wood mice are very good climbers.

Baby mice in a nest.

Wood mouse

Found in countryside and in gardens, the wood mouse eats mainly seeds and insects which it finds at night.

Squirrels eat nuts.

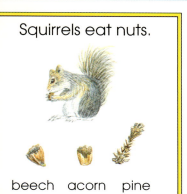

beech   acorn   pine

A squirrel's nest, or drey.

Footprints

Grey Squirrel

Squirrels live in parks, gardens and woods. They bury food to store it for winter, but usually forget where !

Rabbits eat grass and other green plants, but

also nibble the bark of young trees.

Baby rabbits outside their burrow.

Footprin

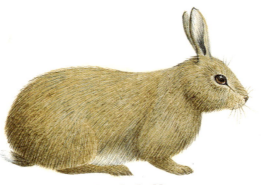

Rabbit

Rabbits live together in warrens. They can be seen feeding beside hedges and in fields at dawn and at dusk.

Hares boxing.

Hares hide in grass in the daytime.

Footprints

Brown hare

Hares live in open country, and are best watched when they feed, at dawn or dusk. They can run very fast.

The earthworm is the shrew's main food.

Female with her nest and young. Shrews live mainly underground.

Common shrew

Shrews live in hedges, fields and woods. If two meet they squeak fiercely, and are often heard fighting.

Male

Slow worms are lizards, not snakes.

Eggs

The young have golden yellow backs.

Female

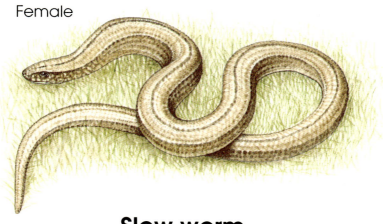

Slow worm

Slow worms are found on sunny slopes, where there are rocks and grass to hide in. They eat mainly slugs.

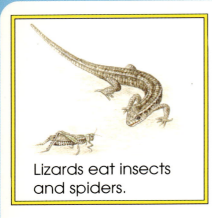

Lizards eat insects and spiders.

Females are fatter than males.

Baby lizards are black.

Male

Common lizard

Lizards live in heathland, sand-dunes and on grassy banks. They like to sunbathe. In winter they hibernate.

Life cycle

Eggs or spawn ⟹ Tadpole ⟹ Young frog

Common frog

Frogs live in moist places, and lay their eggs in ponds. They eat slugs, snails and insects. Frogs can breathe in water.

A toad waits for insects to pounce on.

Eggs or spawn

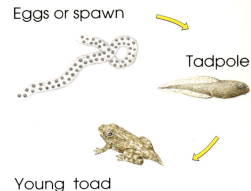

Tadpole

Young toad

Common toad

Toads, like frogs, lay eggs in water. They walk and do not hop. They are often found in gardens in dry places.

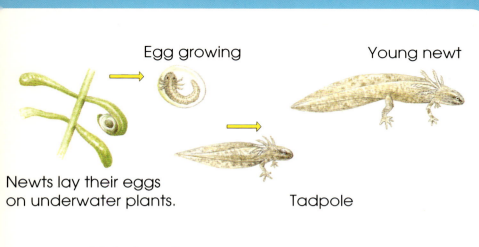

Egg growing

Young newt

Newts lay their eggs
on underwater plants.

Tadpole

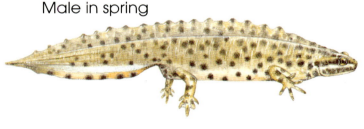

Male in spring

Smooth newt

Newts live in ponds in spring,
but on land at other times.
They catch worms, slugs and
insects at night.

Field voles eat grass.

Many are eaten by kestrels.

Nest and young

Field vole

Voles live in rough grass, and are often heard squeaking. They nest under logs and rocks, even under snow.

Rats eat anything!

The young are blind and naked.

Brown rat

Rats live in buildings, farms, hedges and sewers. They spread disease and cause damage to buildings by gnawing and burrowing.

Hunting worms at night.

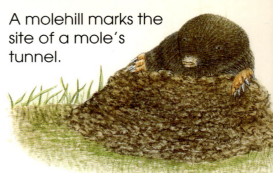
A molehill marks the site of a mole's tunnel.

Mole

Moles live mainly underground and are rarely seen. But their molehills, made when moles tunnel, are a common sight.